THIS REPTILE CARE RECORD BOOK BELONGS TO

_____

First edition: 2019

Insert
Photo

PET INFO	
Name	
Breed	
Date of Birth	
Color	
Special Markings	
Allergies / Illnesses	
Behavior Info	
Feeding Instructions	
Other Notes	

Insert Photo

PET INFO	
Name	
Breed	
Date of Birth	
Color	
Special Markings	
Allergies / Illnesses	
Behavior Info	
Feeding Instructions	
Other Notes	

```
Insert
Photo
```

PET INFO	
Name	
Breed	
Date of Birth	
Color	
Special Markings	
Allergies / Illnesses	
Behavior Info	
Feeding Instructions	
Other Notes	

Insert Photo

PET INFO

Name	
Breed	
Date of Birth	
Color	
Special Markings	
Allergies / Illnesses	
Behavior Info	
Feeding Instructions	
Other Notes	

Insert Photo

PET INFO

Name	
Breed	
Date of Birth	
Color	
Special Markings	
Allergies / Illnesses	
Behavior Info	
Feeding Instructions	
Other Notes	

Insert Photo

PET INFO	
Name	
Breed	
Date of Birth	
Color	
Special Markings	
Allergies / Illnesses	
Behavior Info	
Feeding Instructions	
Other Notes	

Notes

Daily Care Log

Date : _____

FEEDINGS			
Pet	Food	Total	Finished

CLEANINGS		
Pet	BM/Urine	Bath Time

ADDITIONAL RECORD & REMINDER	

Notes

Daily Care Log

Date : _____

FEEDINGS

Pet	Food	Total	Finished

CLEANINGS

Pet	BM/Urine	Bath Time

ADDITIONAL RECORD & REMINDER

Notes

Daily Care Log

Date : _____

FEEDINGS			
Pet	Food	Total	Finished

CLEANINGS		
Pet	BM/Urine	Bath Time

ADDITIONAL RECORD & REMINDER	

Notes

Daily Care Log   Date : _____

FEEDINGS			
Pet	Food	Total	Finished

CLEANINGS		
Pet	BM/Urine	Bath Time

ADDITIONAL RECORD & REMINDER	

Notes

Daily Care Log

Date : _____

FEEDINGS

Pet	Food	Total	Finished

CLEANINGS

Pet	BM/Urine	Bath Time

ADDITIONAL RECORD & REMINDER

Notes

Daily Care Log

Date : _____

FEEDINGS

Pet	Food	Total	Finished

CLEANINGS

Pet	BM/Urine	Bath Time

ADDITIONAL RECORD & REMINDER

Notes

Daily Care Log

Date : _____

FEEDINGS

Pet	Food	Total	Finished

CLEANINGS

Pet	BM/Urine	Bath Time

ADDITIONAL RECORD & REMINDER

Notes

Daily Care Log   Date : _____

FEEDINGS			
Pet	Food	Total	Finished

CLEANINGS		
Pet	BM/Urine	Bath Time

ADDITIONAL RECORD & REMINDER	

Notes

Daily Care Log   Date : _____

FEEDINGS

Pet	Food	Total	Finished

CLEANINGS

Pet	BM/Urine	Bath Time

ADDITIONAL RECORD & REMINDER

Notes

_____

_____

_____

_____

_____

_____

_____

_____

_____

_____

_____

_____

_____

_____

_____

_____

_____

Daily Care Log

Date : _____

FEEDINGS

Pet	Food	Total	Finished

CLEANINGS

Pet	BM/Urine	Bath Time

ADDITIONAL RECORD & REMINDER

Notes

Daily Care Log   Date : _____

FEEDINGS			
Pet	Food	Total	Finished

CLEANINGS		
Pet	BM/Urine	Bath Time

ADDITIONAL RECORD & REMINDER	

Notes

_____

_____

_____

_____

_____

_____

_____

_____

_____

_____

_____

_____

_____

_____

_____

_____

_____

_____

_____

Daily Care Log

Date : _____

FEEDINGS			
Pet	Food	Total	Finished

CLEANINGS		
Pet	BM/Urine	Bath Time

ADDITIONAL RECORD & REMINDER	

Notes

_____

_____

_____

_____

_____

_____

_____

_____

_____

_____

_____

_____

_____

_____

_____

_____

Daily Care Log

Date : _____

FEEDINGS			
Pet	Food	Total	Finished

CLEANINGS		
Pet	BM/Urine	Bath Time

ADDITIONAL RECORD & REMINDER	

Notes

_____
_____
_____
_____
_____
_____
_____
_____
_____
_____
_____
_____
_____
_____
_____
_____
_____
_____
_____
_____
_____
_____

Daily Care Log

Date : _____

FEEDINGS

Pet	Food	Total	Finished

CLEANINGS

Pet	BM/Urine	Bath Time

ADDITIONAL RECORD & REMINDER

Notes

Daily Care Log

Date : _____

FEEDINGS			
Pet	Food	Total	Finished

CLEANINGS		
Pet	BM/Urine	Bath Time

ADDITIONAL RECORD & REMINDER	

Notes

_____

_____

_____

_____

_____

_____

_____

_____

_____

_____

_____

_____

_____

_____

_____

_____

_____

_____

_____

Daily Care Log　　Date : _____

FEEDINGS			
Pet	Food	Total	Finished

CLEANINGS		
Pet	BM/Urine	Bath Time

ADDITIONAL RECORD & REMINDER	

Notes

Daily Care Log

Date : _____

FEEDINGS

Pet	Food	Total	Finished

CLEANINGS

Pet	BM/Urine	Bath Time

ADDITIONAL RECORD & REMINDER

Notes

Daily Care Log   Date : _____

FEEDINGS

Pet	Food	Total	Finished

CLEANINGS

Pet	BM/Urine	Bath Time

ADDITIONAL RECORD & REMINDER

Notes

_____

_____

_____

_____

_____

_____

_____

_____

_____

_____

_____

_____

_____

_____

_____

_____

Daily Care Log

Date : _____

FEEDINGS

Pet	Food	Total	Finished

CLEANINGS

Pet	BM/Urine	Bath Time

ADDITIONAL RECORD & REMINDER

Notes

Daily Care Log

Date : _____

FEEDINGS

Pet	Food	Total	Finished

CLEANINGS

Pet	BM/Urine	Bath Time

ADDITIONAL RECORD & REMINDER

Notes

Daily Care Log

Date : _____

FEEDINGS			
Pet	Food	Total	Finished

CLEANINGS		
Pet	BM/Urine	Bath Time

ADDITIONAL RECORD & REMINDER	

Notes

_____

_____

_____

_____

_____

_____

_____

_____

_____

_____

_____

_____

_____

_____

_____

_____

_____

Daily Care Log   Date : _____

FEEDINGS

Pet	Food	Total	Finished

CLEANINGS

Pet	BM/Urine	Bath Time

ADDITIONAL RECORD & REMINDER

Notes

Daily Care Log   Date : _____

FEEDINGS			
Pet	Food	Total	Finished

CLEANINGS		
Pet	BM/Urine	Bath Time

ADDITIONAL RECORD & REMINDER	

Notes

_____

_____

_____

_____

_____

_____

_____

_____

_____

_____

_____

_____

_____

_____

_____

_____

Daily Care Log

Date : _____

FEEDINGS			
Pet	Food	Total	Finished

CLEANINGS		
Pet	BM/Urine	Bath Time

ADDITIONAL RECORD & REMINDER	

Notes

Daily Care Log

Date : _____

FEEDINGS			
Pet	Food	Total	Finished

CLEANINGS		
Pet	BM/Urine	Bath Time

ADDITIONAL RECORD & REMINDER	

Notes

_____
_____
_____
_____
_____
_____
_____
_____
_____
_____
_____
_____
_____
_____
_____
_____

Daily Care Log

Date : _____

FEEDINGS			
Pet	Food	Total	Finished

CLEANINGS		
Pet	BM/Urine	Bath Time

ADDITIONAL RECORD & REMINDER	

Notes

Daily Care Log

Date : _____

FEEDINGS

Pet	Food	Total	Finished

CLEANINGS

Pet	BM/Urine	Bath Time

ADDITIONAL RECORD & REMINDER

Notes

_____

_____

_____

_____

_____

_____

_____

_____

_____

_____

_____

_____

_____

_____

_____

_____

_____

_____

_____

Daily Care Log

Date : _____

FEEDINGS

Pet	Food	Total	Finished

CLEANINGS

Pet	BM/Urine	Bath Time

ADDITIONAL RECORD & REMINDER

Notes

_____

_____

_____

_____

_____

_____

_____

_____

_____

_____

_____

_____

_____

_____

_____

Daily Care Log

Date : _____

FEEDINGS

Pet	Food	Total	Finished

CLEANINGS

Pet	BM/Urine	Bath Time

ADDITIONAL RECORD & REMINDER

Notes

Daily Care Log   Date : _____

FEEDINGS

Pet	Food	Total	Finished

CLEANINGS

Pet	BM/Urine	Bath Time

ADDITIONAL RECORD & REMINDER

Notes

Daily Care Log

Date : _____

FEEDINGS			
Pet	Food	Total	Finished

CLEANINGS		
Pet	BM/Urine	Bath Time

ADDITIONAL RECORD & REMINDER	

Notes

_____

_____

_____

_____

_____

_____

_____

_____

_____

_____

_____

_____

_____

_____

_____

_____

_____

_____

Daily Care Log

Date : _____

FEEDINGS

Pet	Food	Total	Finished

CLEANINGS

Pet	BM/Urine	Bath Time

ADDITIONAL RECORD & REMINDER

Notes

Daily Care Log

Date : _____

FEEDINGS			
Pet	Food	Total	Finished

CLEANINGS		
Pet	BM/Urine	Bath Time

ADDITIONAL RECORD & REMINDER	

Notes

_____
_____
_____
_____
_____
_____
_____
_____
_____
_____
_____
_____
_____
_____
_____
_____
_____
_____
_____
_____
_____

Daily Care Log   Date : _____

FEEDINGS

Pet	Food	Total	Finished

CLEANINGS

Pet	BM/Urine	Bath Time

ADDITIONAL RECORD & REMINDER

Notes

Daily Care Log

Date : _____

FEEDINGS			
Pet	Food	Total	Finished

CLEANINGS		
Pet	BM/Urine	Bath Time

ADDITIONAL RECORD & REMINDER	

Notes

_____

_____

_____

_____

_____

_____

_____

_____

_____

_____

_____

_____

_____

_____

_____

_____

_____

_____

Daily Care Log   Date : _____

FEEDINGS

Pet	Food	Total	Finished

CLEANINGS

Pet	BM/Urine	Bath Time

ADDITIONAL RECORD & REMINDER

Notes

Daily Care Log   Date : _____

FEEDINGS			
Pet	Food	Total	Finished

CLEANINGS		
Pet	BM/Urine	Bath Time

ADDITIONAL RECORD & REMINDER	

Notes

_____

_____

_____

_____

_____

_____

_____

_____

_____

_____

_____

_____

_____

_____

_____

_____

_____

_____

Daily Care Log

Date : _____

FEEDINGS			
Pet	Food	Total	Finished

CLEANINGS		
Pet	BM/Urine	Bath Time

ADDITIONAL RECORD & REMINDER	

Notes

Daily Care Log

Date : _____

FEEDINGS			
Pet	Food	Total	Finished

CLEANINGS		
Pet	BM/Urine	Bath Time

ADDITIONAL RECORD & REMINDER	

Notes

_____
_____
_____
_____
_____
_____
_____
_____
_____
_____
_____
_____
_____
_____
_____
_____
_____
_____
_____
_____

Daily Care Log   Date : _____

FEEDINGS			
Pet	Food	Total	Finished

CLEANINGS		
Pet	BM/Urine	Bath Time

ADDITIONAL RECORD & REMINDER	

Notes

Daily Care Log

Date : _____

FEEDINGS

Pet	Food	Total	Finished

CLEANINGS

Pet	BM/Urine	Bath Time

ADDITIONAL RECORD & REMINDER

Notes

Daily Care Log

Date : _____

FEEDINGS

Pet	Food	Total	Finished

CLEANINGS

Pet	BM/Urine	Bath Time

ADDITIONAL RECORD & REMINDER

Notes

Daily Care Log

Date : _____

FEEDINGS

Pet	Food	Total	Finished

CLEANINGS

Pet	BM/Urine	Bath Time

ADDITIONAL RECORD & REMINDER

Notes

_____

_____

_____

_____

_____

_____

_____

_____

_____

_____

_____

_____

_____

_____

_____

_____

_____

_____

_____

_____

_____

Daily Care Log

Date : _____

FEEDINGS

Pet	Food	Total	Finished

CLEANINGS

Pet	BM/Urine	Bath Time

ADDITIONAL RECORD & REMINDER

Notes

Daily Care Log   Date : _____

FEEDINGS			
Pet	Food	Total	Finished

CLEANINGS		
Pet	BM/Urine	Bath Time

ADDITIONAL RECORD & REMINDER	

Notes

_____

_____

_____

_____

_____

_____

_____

_____

_____

_____

_____

_____

_____

_____

_____

_____

_____

_____

_____

Daily Care Log

Date : _____

FEEDINGS			
Pet	Food	Total	Finished

CLEANINGS		
Pet	BM/Urine	Bath Time

ADDITIONAL RECORD & REMINDER	

Notes

Daily Care Log

Date : _____

FEEDINGS

Pet	Food	Total	Finished

CLEANINGS

Pet	BM/Urine	Bath Time

ADDITIONAL RECORD & REMINDER

Notes

Daily Care Log

Date : _____

FEEDINGS

Pet	Food	Total	Finished

CLEANINGS

Pet	BM/Urine	Bath Time

ADDITIONAL RECORD & REMINDER

Notes

Daily Care Log

Date : _____

FEEDINGS			
Pet	Food	Total	Finished

CLEANINGS		
Pet	BM/Urine	Bath Time

ADDITIONAL RECORD & REMINDER	

Notes

_____

_____

_____

_____

_____

_____

_____

_____

_____

_____

_____

_____

_____

_____

_____

_____

_____

_____

_____

Daily Care Log

Date : _____

FEEDINGS			
Pet	Food	Total	Finished

CLEANINGS		
Pet	BM/Urine	Bath Time

ADDITIONAL RECORD & REMINDER	

Notes

Daily Care Log   Date : _____

FEEDINGS

Pet	Food	Total	Finished

CLEANINGS

Pet	BM/Urine	Bath Time

ADDITIONAL RECORD & REMINDER

Notes

Daily Care Log

Date : _____

FEEDINGS

Pet	Food	Total	Finished

CLEANINGS

Pet	BM/Urine	Bath Time

ADDITIONAL RECORD & REMINDER

Notes

Daily Care Log

Date : _____

FEEDINGS

Pet	Food	Total	Finished

CLEANINGS

Pet	BM/Urine	Bath Time

ADDITIONAL RECORD & REMINDER

Notes

Daily Care Log

Date : _____

FEEDINGS

Pet	Food	Total	Finished

CLEANINGS

Pet	BM/Urine	Bath Time

ADDITIONAL RECORD & REMINDER

Notes

Daily Care Log

Date : _____

FEEDINGS			
Pet	Food	Total	Finished

CLEANINGS		
Pet	BM/Urine	Bath Time

ADDITIONAL RECORD & REMINDER	

Notes

_____

_____

_____

_____

_____

_____

_____

_____

_____

_____

_____

_____

_____

_____

_____

_____

_____

_____

_____

Daily Care Log

Date : _____

FEEDINGS			
Pet	Food	Total	Finished

CLEANINGS		
Pet	BM/Urine	Bath Time

ADDITIONAL RECORD & REMINDER	

Notes

CPSIA information can be obtained
at www.ICGtesting.com
Printed in the USA
BVHW011013101021
618623BV00014B/987

9 781086 317251